MUSIC
and the
LINE OF MOST RESISTANCE

By Artur Schnabel

In these lectures, Artur Schnabel ranges
philosophically over every aspect of music
— history, influence, the function of composers, performers and teachers. But re-
current throughout is the point that the
musician in all his functions must serve also
as a communicator via the written and
spoken word.
Communication on music takes many
forms: instructions from composer to performer, from conductor to orchestra, from
teacher to student; annotations to programs and new editions; speeches and
articles by composers, performers and amateurs; and, of major import, reviews by
the critics. Schnabel defines, categorizes,
explains, bewails, and waxes philosophical
on these forms of communication while dis-
cussing their function.
Renowned as a pianist for his interpretations of Beethoven and Schubert over a
period of fifty years, Schnabel speaks with
authority and clarity on his subject. Musicians and laymen alike will find in these
lectures many provocative and stimulating
ideas.

MUSIC
AND THE LINE OF
MOST RESISTANCE

(0)

Da Capo Press Music Reprint Series

GENERAL EDITOR

FREDERICK FREEDMAN

VASSAR COLLEGE

MUSIC
AND THE LINE OF
MOST RESISTANCE

BY ARTUR SCHNABEL

DA CAPO PRESS · NEW YORK · 1969

A Da Capo Press Reprint Edition

This Da Capo Press edition of
Music and the Line of Most Resistance
is an unabridged republication of the
first edition published in 1942. It
is reprinted by special arrangement
with Princeton University Press.

Library of Congress Catalog Card Number 69-12690

Published by Da Capo Press
A Division of Plenum Publishing Corporation
227 West 17th Street
New York, N.Y. 10011
Printed in the United States of America

MUSIC AND THE LINE OF
MOST RESISTANCE

Music

and the line of most resistance

BY

ARTUR SCHNABEL

Princeton, New Jersey

PRINCETON UNIVERSITY PRESS

1942

PREFACE

What is printed in this little volume is the result of my first thoroughgoing attempt —aside from letters—at writing (and thinking) in English. I therefore ask the reader's indulgence if now and again my use of the language betrays the fact that it is not my mother tongue.

The text as published here is the text of three lectures given in April 1940 at the University of Chicago. For valuable linguistic advice I feel gratefully obliged to Mr. John U. Nef, Mr. Cesar Saerchinger, and Mr. Roger Sessions.

A. S.

MUSIC AND THE LINE OF
MOST RESISTANCE

I am a musician—a professional musician. The activities of a musician, as he is represented in our civilization, are: writing music, performing music, and teaching how to read, write and perform music. The musician who writes music has no compelling reason to talk about music, but even he cannot dispense with the assistance of words. To the music he has added some words which indicate to the performer how to interpret the written music; for instance, the "tempo" (which after the invention of the metronome could be also given in figures), the sonority, and the character of expression. In short, all those elements inseparable from a musical performance to which the notation of music is not applicable, must be communicated by the medium of words. Music, for the technique of performance, is forced to borrow from the word language except when the composer of the music reserves for himself the monopoly of performance, and then only in the case of an absolute solo.

The musician who performs music has a choice among numerous tone-sounding instruments. On most of these instruments he can execute only one tone at a time, but he can produce in succession, of course, all the single tones within the range of his instrument. On string instruments the player can execute several tones simultaneously; on the piano—the largest of them—as many as ten fingers allow; on the organ, with its devices of coupling and pedalling, many more.

A solo performer who executes all the tones of a piece of music has no more reason to talk about music than has the writer of the music. The performer is concerned with words only when he observes the interpretative hints given in word symbols by the composer. A performance demanding several players, i.e. an ensemble, already requires a greater employment of words. In a small ensemble up to—let me say—eight players, this use of words takes the form of a discussion. The players exchange suggestions in order to achieve unanimity of conception, adjustment of means and the adequate distribution of weights.

Performances by larger ensembles—by orchestras, choirs, and in the theater—require one musician who directs the others, but who does not himself play an instrument in the performances. He, the conductor, is a cross between performer and teacher. He is not quite a performer, for others have to materialize his interpretation on their instruments; and he is not quite a teacher, because the instrumentalists, in a respectable professional ensemble, need no other instruction than that of referring to the conductor's conception of the piece. Also, in sharp contrast to the music teacher whose function it is to try to inspire, the conductor tries to limit the performer's free display of individuality. He has to do that. A great number of players—even good and very experienced players—left free to do what each of them feels (particularly in a work not familiar to them as an ensemble), might easily produce some rather unpleasant disorder. On the other hand it has often happened that a body of not too highly gifted, not very advanced players, stimulated and elevated by a great artist who demanded more of them than they would ever have trusted themselves to do alone, has accomplished performances of a pure and exciting quality approaching perfection.

Orchestras, choruses and, to a certain extent also the singers of solo parts in operas and oratorios, have no choice but to follow their conductor's command. Even the musician who executes the solo part in a concerto, which he knows inside out, in many cases much better than the conductor knows it, has to abandon a varying amount of his freedom, though actually his line and lead should be accepted for such a work. A good conductor, in any case, will release more than he suppresses. The importance of the performer's "personality" is generally very much overrated, and must, in all team work at least, be controlled.

Experiments have been made in orchestral performances without the guidance of a conductor. I heard concerts given by such a group in Moscow in 1925. It would, of course, have been more interesting and instructive to be present at their rehearsals.

The men, all expert players, were seated in a circle facing each other as if at a round table, but without the table. The first passages sounded most impressive as a technical feat, astonishing as a triumph of drill. But soon the performance became more and more stiff, mechanical, lifeless, fixed to one straight flat track, excluding spontaneity and ease. And, by the way, there was one among them who regulated the "traffic"—a secret concealed conductor—and there was a system of signalling "nuances" as well. It may be that the details of the performance had been decided by vote. It was still necessary for the players to warn each other at dangerous points. To me the whole adventure seemed pointless, inartistic and artificial. True, the actual, proper conductor, he who plays with only a stick in the air (though now even that toneless instrument has often been sacrificed in favor of hands, arms or other mute but eloquent parts of the body), appears at a fairly late stage in the history of musical performances. He became necessary with the growth in size of orchestras. He appeared because the old way of making the players play together in time and spirit had proved insufficient. Someone was needed in order to tell them how to proceed and succeed.

Before I come to the musician who teaches I must mention especially the musician who writes and the musician who performs vocal music, because of their particular connection with words, the closest to which musicians can arrive. The reasons for writing vocal music are many and manifold. The voice being the primary musical instrument, tradition is probably the strongest motive. The next strongest are the sensuousness, spontaneity, direct emotional expressiveness of the human voice—qualities which no other instrument can substitute or rival. Words, if they are descriptive, may inspire the musical imagination. They provide an atmosphere or tendency to the writer of the music and facilitate the performer's and the listener's approach to it. Individual and social functions, private and public life, intimacy and festivity—all demand the comforting or exalting concurrence of the liberated voice or voices, which always insures an incomparably genuine and personal touch. There is also the possibility of innumerable performances, since everybody possesses the vocal instrument, the habit of using it, and to some degree also the technique for using it.

Man's voice, a complex part of his organism, produces speech as well as song, which may have been identical in the beginning. The line of demarcation was drawn when tones, losing their qualification as mere tones with a definite pitch, and thus essentially altered, were used for the formation of words. Words are compounds of tones. To make these compounds intelligible, consonants—which are not tones but results of tongue and lip movements—were interposed as suitable links and indispensable auxiliary sounds. What amazing genius! The compounds are entities, units, apparently contrived as vehicles to convey ideas, whereas previously applied devices of communication (mere tones, for instance) had become too limited. Here probably begins the end of the use of mere tones for the purpose of communication. Today, with loudspeakers, amplifiers and sirens, mere tones will also soon be dismissed from the last positions they still hold as announcers and callers.

Tones as mere tones, and arranged as movement of tones, were, after the creation of words, confined to a region of their own—to song. The medium of music was established, a prerequisite of which, I repeat, is the juxtaposition of several successive tones. It is not music's function to express rational necessities. The human spirit has commissioned the human voice to appear in two languages. One to serve man's intellect and purpose; the other to serve his sentiment and his transcendental urge. Both enter incessantly into man's consciousness. Words call for utterance, when someone is to be addressed. A partner is wanted; soliloquies are rare. But tones are emitted in solitude, in small or numerous company. Many can sing simultaneously different tones in different rhythmical order, so long as pitch and meter are given; but words spoken by a chorus must be in uniform rhythm and intervals in order to be comprehensible. Song depends on tone exclusively, not at all on words; speech, however, is not meant to be music. Song and speech can coincide; vocally produced tones are automatically also parts of words.

No man-made instrument can speak words. (I don't wish to enter the realm of electrically produced sounds.) Most of all vocal music is equipped with words, or fitted to them, if you like. The author of such music, and each singer who performs it, is inevitably concerned with words and what they represent, much more than his colleagues in the nonvocal provinces of music. But such employment of words with music is very different from the use of words in talking about music. For talk about music the singer has just as little cause as have other musicians.

After the separation of vocal expression into tone-language and word-language, these two entities, which are capable of independent existence, were fused into a third entity. This new, combined language comprises word-language only in part, but tone-language in its entirety. With its rational, purposeful, utilitarian aims, word-language must have failed to satisfy some of the human impulses of expression, the poetical and mystical ambitions of man. To compensate for this lack, word-language was driven again and again to music with words, even after glorious attempts to become self-sufficient. Incidentally, one type of musical piece is named "song without words," though words are in no way an inherent element of song. The name surely is an unmeditated tribute to a practice. In music with words, only those elements of word-language have been united with music which are striving for sublimity, or at least emphasis. This statement may seem strange to many when one thinks of the stupid, shabby and vulgar words of most of the popular songs of the day. Yet, even here, the words are still picked from somewhere in the vicinity of poetry. Serious contemporary musicians, surrealists, have assumed the prerogative of breaking this old rule. Reports from the cattle market, police decrees, and similar mundane stuff have been chosen by them as words to their songs. This snobbish joke did not last.

The problem of how to sing mere commentary or realistic colloquial talk has been solved in operas and oratorios, as you all know, by the introduction of the so-called recitative, later extended to *Sprechgesang* (speech-song). In this the tempo and inflections of speech are retained in spite of being fixed to certain tones. And only in the recitative has speech preserved some of its own power of communication. It has been observed and proved that in other combinations of words and tones the musical element always appears to be the master. Words are deprived of their sovereignty.

As I have indicated before, it must be a very ancient custom to use music as a background to various situations in human life. The types of music created for different occasions must have been recognizably distinct from each other, in accordance with the specific demands of the situation. The prayer, the lullaby, the war song—each had its own musical significance. In any of these types of music the significance is not lost or even weakened or altered if alien words—words not belonging to them—are uttered, or no words at all. You may sing about a hare in a largo, or of a snail in a presto piece. This is absurd if you think about it. If the music is agreeable to you, it remains agreeable whatever the words. We must, nevertheless, demand and expect an ideal and material correspondence of words and tones, for deliberate meaninglessness is an inefficient and offensive trick, even when it contains some amusing moments. The adequacy of the words is—morally, so to speak—a justified supposition, and these words, if you give them separate consideration, will immediately regain their importance; when used in connection with music, however, they are doomed to comparative irrelevance.

The music, then, provides the significance, and as long as the one type of music is heard it will not be confused with another type, not even when unsuitable words are added to it. Could anyone, after seeing announced in a program a solemn, tragic funeral march, followed by the lines of a gloomy poem, believe he is actually hearing the funeral march, even though in its place, without notice, an exactly opposite type of music should be performed—say a galop or a jig? On the other hand, does a person, mentally hearing such a grouping of tones, which he has always heard in connection with certain words, automatically remember the words as well? Or does he remember them when he whistles or is humming the music? (The faculty of whistling is, to a degree, similar to that of singing. That no noun, no name exists for the instrument by which we produce whistled tones, is strange. The coincidence of words and whistled tones is also not quite impossible, though I don't imagine that many will think of trying this technique. Some whistlers are even able to produce two tones at once.)

The performer of a song, to be true, is often induced to stress some single, strongly descriptive words among those he is singing, without regard for the musical line which might forbid the accents he gives. Tone groups may appear imitative or indicative; they are never genuinely, originally or exactly descriptive. Hearing a run, you might associate it with God knows what! A performer's exaggeration in underlining the words, and thus, perhaps, distorting the music, nevertheless will have to go very far before it can rob the music of its supremacy, or relegate the music to second place. If he succeeds, the listener might be irritated rather than delighted, and might criticize the singer for being an actor.

Cheap music set to noble words exposes the cheapness of the music; beautiful and profound music set to insignificant words still communicates the beauty of the music. Music is not suited to the rôle of a servant; it is never subordinated except in cases of diminished auditory perception. If the hearer's optical sense is absorbed, however, music is degraded to a position of a more or less conspicuous helpmate. This can be experienced at the cinema, for example, where even musical masterpieces become insignificant. Music which accompanies physical activity suffers the same fate. Music as music can be absorbed only in a state of physical passivity. Words as words never directly arouse sensuous reactions; thus they cannot impair the superiority of music which addresses itself to the ear without appealing simultaneously to the intellect. The gradual recognition of this superiority must have been important in the eventual development of the autonomy of music.

Now, after a lengthy detour, I come to the type of musician who teaches how to write, read and perform music. The teacher's work demands a considerably more extensive use of words than does that of the composer and the performer. The teacher also occasionally uses many of the sorts of paraphrase which, in the big enterprise of music, are entrusted to those functionaries who only talk, the people whose endeavors circle round about music, who try to penetrate into it from the outside, who reflect and report in general and in particular on all musical products and affairs, but who are not among the makers of these products. These—the makers—have to travel the opposite route, from the interior to the exterior, from conception to appearance, from idea to shape. The teacher is sharply distinguished from the illustrators, nomenclators, hermeneutists and philosophers by his determination to transform immediately and permanently everything he teaches into written or performed music. It is his business to introduce his disciples to actual music-making (or musical realization), from the initial steps on a restricted plane to the loftiest flights within the musical cosmos; in other words, from technique to mystery. He has to present the whole course, from seemingly simple and modest aspirations by way of increasing (even frightening) complications toward a higher, a second simplicity, toward that other shore which, to be sure, can only be sighted but never reached.

Needless to say, I do not mean to assign to any one teacher the job of imparting all stages of the totality of music (which, after all, will remain unknown in any case); nor do I credit all students with the capacity of absorbing all there is to music. As in other courses of training, the teacher who gives the final courses is not the one who gives the first. Even if one person could do both, which I doubt, it would certainly be wasteful. You don't employ a mountain guide to teach babies to walk.

I have already said that the music teacher is compelled to talk a great deal more than the composer and the performer who are direct producers of music. He must teach accepted rules which are derived from an accumulation of past musical activities. The teacher, being neither just an historian nor an analyst, begins with the synthesis of musical knowledge which has been reached at his time. His program is limited by the conventions and conveniences of his age. (How these conventions are formed is rather a riddle. Probably many of them are accidental.) The fact has to be accepted that normally only a very small part of old substance (of musical literature) and only a very small part of the contemporary product is comprised in the music teacher's repertoire. This repertoire, of course, changes with every generation, or even faster, though only very slightly so. The inertia of established rules has enormous power of resistance, and who knows whether such toughness is to be deplored or welcomed? Traditions, as in other fields, must not be condemned altogether on the ground that some might be obsolete and some even false.

The student who is training to write music wants, comparatively speaking, but little tuition. Every writer of music—I think one can say without exception—begins his musical study by learning to play an instrument. So does every student who is destined to become a conductor or a music teacher. Students of composition have to become acquainted with numerous different ways of arranging their material, exemplified by the musical works of earlier periods and by more or less important innovations of more recent times, chosen always within the horizon of contemporary views. They have to acquire the knowledge of how to treat different instruments, again by examples; and they have to prove their understanding of the discipline by actual attempts at composition, moving from the simplest to more and more exacting patterns.

Traces of originality, of differences in talents and types of talents, can be noticed in the early stages of such exercises. Even if only a minimum of freedom is granted, one student will scarcely ever solve the problems at hand in exactly the same manner as any other student. This proves that music, apart from a few elementary and arbitrary stipulations, is not as fixed as the multiplication table. Nor has the classification of right or wrong any validity for music, which is beyond being measured and judged by quantity or by "moral" standards.

The aptitudes shown by beginners are no guarantee of future accomplishment. An apparently stubborn child may later on surpass by far his schoolmates who, at the outset, have shown greater facility and cleverness. Practically all musicians except singers—amateurs and professionals alike—get their first training as children. Singers are different in this respect, because their instrument, the voice, reaches a settled condition only after adolescence. Another reason is that one does not need a teacher to sing. Human beings sing naturally at an age when it would be impossible to learn how to use another instrument. Besides, a voice is not just a *musical* gift. Voice is not identical with imagination or even with ambition. One distinguishes between ugly and beautiful voices. Having one or the other is a physiological accident. No musical performer, save the singer, becomes a musical performer simply because he possesses an instrument. You or your father can buy any man-made instrument, but nobody can buy or hire a "voice."

Every music student should be obliged to write music, whether or not he is gifted for it or attracted by it. Such an obligation is, unfortunately, not even recommended nowadays, although it was a matter of course in former times. Today the instrumental or vocal student gets, in addition to his principal training, some incidental instruction in the so-called theory of music which, though necessary for the composer, is only of slight help to the performer. It might be a great help in the development of performers, however, if they were to experiment in composition, or if their knowledge of theory would at least be completed and strengthened by the copying of music written by others.

The student who learns to perform needs a great amount of information as well as training. He has to labor physically to cause his instrument to sound. (It goes without saying that here the singer is no exception, although at the same time there are essential differences.) With a man-made instrument, an inanimate bulk, pleasant and unpleasant effects can be obtained. It operates as though it wished to co-operate. Such man-made instruments are not identical, even if made by the same hands or the same machines at the same period, according to the same methods and with similar materials. But the best and the worst of them react to the handling they enjoy or suffer. And, strangely enough, they might in effect become almost equal if the superior one is used to its minimum capacity and the inferior one to its maximum.

The prospective performer has to labor mentally to comprehend the finished piece of music which he undertakes to transform into sounding reality, to comprehend it not merely as an arrangement of tones, but as a formed and organized expression. His teacher must direct him methodically through this multitude of requirements, must guide his instinct, release his emotion and intelligence, without restricting his urge for freedom. And, ultimately, he has to be careful to mould the student's ambition, concentration and exertion into a permanent, increasing, inspiring and conscious joy. It is of the greatest importance, especially for the student performer, to know that the words written to music and almost all words spoken by the teacher during the lessons, are mere tools. Only the end to which they have been the means, the realization in sounding tones, must be in the mind of a performer in action. The words as such ought to be completely forgotten. They originated in a recognition of musical forms and the minutest details of musical form, and they serve as messengers to convey orders and advice from this recognition to the performer. Descriptive and prescriptive words, in themselves essentially alien to the music, have been inserted for a transient purpose. When the execution of those orders starts, the messenger must disappear.

A very small portion of the vocabulary is used for these directions, and although most of these few words have several meanings and applications, the musician will always choose the meaning which relates to music. Thus, in writing and performing music, musical ideas and intentions must precede the appearance of the music itself.

The writer of music is absolutely free to interrupt the train of his musical ideas, whatever may motivate the interruption. He may proceed from one part of the piece on which he is at work to the next or to any other part quite at will. (Mozart often composed different works simultaneously, working now on one, now on the other in mixed order.) It might take a composer a whole year to write a piece which, when performed, lasts only a few minutes. Yet each passage he writes is necessarily preceded by a musical idea.

But the performer, once he has begun, must not interrupt the train of musical ideas. Only when the musical idea precedes the musical performance can the maximum of concentration, always required, be secured. The less diluted—or polluted—the preceding idea, the steadier will be the concentration.

The precedence of the musical idea is in any case the only judicious approach, because of the singularity of music. Music has to be inspired, regulated and controlled at the same moment by the spiritual and the physical ear, as one organ representing the composer, conductor, performer, listener and critic all in one. They all communicate exclusively through the medium of music. Each of these partners might have his share to contribute, now in explanatory words, occasionally in words suggesting a picture which might promote the desired result. The suggestions, however, have an exclusively musical meaning. A conductor may shout "pianissimo please"; or he may whisper in despair, "why don't you play fortissimo?" The rebuked players know what music he wants. When he coldly says "tender" or "gay" or "clouded," the music must be tender or gay or clouded. During the performance he must secure the intended articulation and expression by transmission of the musical idea through musical energy.

There is another reason for excluding words of any sort from the motive power that achieves the performance, namely, the difference in duration between words and tones. The teacher has warned you: "Don't give an accent on this first beat." If you try to remember this whole sentence before delivering this first beat you will have passed the beat before the words have had time to pass through your memory. You start to remember before this contested beat and arrive at the last word after it is all over. Consequently, the neighboring tones of this beat must have been neglected and mechanically executed; the music must have suffered from the uneven treatment of parts of it—where an uneven treatment was not indicated musically. "First hear, then play!" That advice seems paradoxical, and yet it is in the natural order of conception and appearance. It would be a paradox if it were addressed to the listener, who has to be taken from appearance back to conception (another paradox). It is addressed to the performer and to him it is a major command. Just as we can think in words, can recite the words and make the hearer think, so we can think in tones. But thinking in the two languages—speech and music—is not commensurable, and I always hesitate to use the verb "to think" for music, (although all my life I have done practically nothing else than "think" in music), because this word evokes an association with recognition, purpose or judgment.

To have the idea of tone, the idea of a particular arrangement of tones in mind before they are materialized is taken for granted for the writer of music, who materializes his tone-ideas in visible signs. For complete materialization the tone-ideas have to appear in sound. The producer of the sounds cannot always be relied on to have that creative type of idea in mind before he performs music. As I said before, he must have experience with the instrument he uses; and in his endeavor to satisfy the technical demands of his instrument—in order to secure the smooth functioning of his tools—he can easily neglect the creative task, to the extent of obliterating the imaginative side of music, for which even the quintessence of dexterity and an infallible apparatus cannot serve as substitutes. Nor does absolute correctness or strict faithfulness to the visible signs help much, if there is no relationship with the roots of music. The teacher must insist upon the observance of the natural sequence of the elements of performance. He must impress upon the student the axiom that the tonal idea can be efficacious on one single occasion only. Therefore, it has to emerge afresh on each new occasion, and this function can never become automatic.

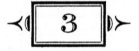

The term musician includes not only professionals but also amateurs in composition and performance. Teaching, of course, is almost exclusively an occupation for professionals. The division into amateurs and professionals is made not on the basis of difference in quality and degree of talent, but on the basis of differences in social background. The musical amateur is a product of the upper class, a kind of intellectual sportsman, if sportsmanship can be separated from competition and fighting. I never know when the term "sport," in the present-day conception of it, is legitimately applied. Is it sport to walk, swim, ride, climb mountains, hunt, fish, sail, etc.? All these activities one can pursue and enjoy alone, and some of them have no other purpose than the pleasure they provide. Or does sport always imply opposition, a test in a match between opponents, a game ending in victory or defeat? Does the game of chess belong to sport? I don't know. But I know that in the realm of music all endeavors are ideally directed toward cooperation, toward the establishment of unity. No musician works against another musician. All efforts to set up records in the sense of competitive sport are essentially foreign to the musician's type of struggle.

The appreciation of and participation in the higher cultural life has always been a pastime and an obligation of the upper class. The men and women of the upper class once had sufficient spare time and sufficient concentration to engage in any attractive, worthy and exacting activity, and their personal prestige was considerably raised by doing so. The children brought up in such a milieu have always been expected and inspired to follow their parents' and ancestors' footsteps; at least, they always had an easy opportunity to become familiar with artistic treasures.

Upper class children with outstanding talent might have been given a more special and thorough training than is usually given and as grownups might have devoted themselves to music more than to other of their inclinations, and yet they did not always become professional musicians. Professional musicians—even those who achieved fame—had, for a long time, no social standing. Any member of the upper class practising music as a profession had to show such unmistakable genius that no alternative was left, otherwise, he would not have been tolerated by his class. (Profession, in that case, is not to be interpreted as a method of making a living, but as a life work which satisfies not only the professional's but other people's desire for contact with music.)

An amateur, then, is by talent, tradition and surroundings a musician who makes his very first acquaintance with music as *art*, as an aspiration of the choicest kind. I do not adhere unreservedly to the so-called milieu theory. Musical talent, like almost any other talent, is manifestly distributed among human beings regardless of social rank. I only wish to point to the fact that the members of the upper class, while they constituted rather a small group, were during the period of their accepted reign the consumers and supporters of art. They appreciated values which rarely were created by them but always, as it were, for them; their own musical activity was an important part of their support.

Not all of them were amateurs, but I think one can say there must have been in every generation of every family one who was naturally equipped to continue the enjoyable privilege and duty of promoting musical culture. The majority of amateurs performed music; those who composed probably did rather modest work, though several attempts have been made in the higher realms, and quite successfully, but whatever the function, it always had some relation to the high standard of "art music" cultivated in their circles. Even the musical patterns for light entertainment in these circles were distinguished from the songs and dances current among the common people. The material for the amateurs' dignified hobbies, as we would nowadays rather frivolously call them, were furnished by professional musicians, mostly of humble origin. Their environment did not encourage esthetic impulses; they became professional musicians, of whatever sort, simply because they were definitely gifted. As professionals they automatically served the wealthy patrons of music.

With the development of music, the services of musicians became more and more diversified. The orchestra, particularly the modern orchestra, be it used for amusement or for exaltation, employs numerous musicians, not all of whom are given parts equally difficult to execute. How musically talented persons and persons attracted to music come to choose a drum as the instrument for displaying their gifts and satisfying their urges seems to me somewhat mysterious. Fortunately, some do choose it, but one cannot presume that it would attract the amateur. And yet, orchestras composed exclusively or partly of amateurs, are not rare—especially since the bourgeoisie joined and later succeeded the nobility in taking charge of music, which then spread beyond court, castle and salon. Such amateur orchestras are to be found chiefly in places where professional orchestras, for economic reasons, cannot exist. Either the places are too small or the inhabitants interested in music not numerous enough to allow the luxury of an orchestra. The old-time Maecenas, who kept his own orchestra and often gave the people free admission to hear this orchestra, gradually disappeared. The people began to pay for hearing music. Except for those employed in the theater, choirs—even the largest ones—were and still are composed mostly of amateurs.

It is doubtful whether in a large professional ensemble every player knows much more than his own part, and whatever happens in the music simultaneously with his part. Singers of operatic rôles, like actors in plays, are more often than not rather ignorant of the scenes in which they are not employed.

If this is not the right attitude, it is an understandable one, for many of the activities referred to contain traits of mere handicraft which can be exercised by trained and moderately-gifted specialists who need not necessarily be very high minded artists. Detachment of that kind has never been the amateur's attitude. His connection with music originates not only in his gift and his training, but chiefly in the desire to come closer and closer to music—to music as a whole. He is quite unselfish in aiming at the solitary happiness to be gained from a voluntary, reverent deed. He need not be concerned with perfection of execution and is not obliged to waste his precious spare time for technical preparation. Even without such technical preparation, he will improve step by step simply by the force of conscientious enthusiasm. The ideal instrument for the amateur is the piano, for which an imposing number of the greatest works are at his disposal. The piano has the advantage that most of the music written for other instruments can be arranged for it with the loss only of the specific sonority of the other instruments—a loss of little importance by comparison with the profit that can be secured. The pianist needs no partner to become acquainted with music. Orchestral scores may be arranged for four hands in order to present the entire musical text.

Since the invention of machines for the reproduction of music, the number of serious amateurs has decreased depressingly. I hope that the phonograph and the radio, which have stopped so many amateurs, have now begun to attract new converts to music. Detailed statistics on this process would be instructive, but thus far are not available. Several

the piano and writing music. When I was twelve years old teaching activities were added and since then have not been interrupted. Some years ago I also did some editing of standard works. In all these fifty years I have neither written nor lectured about music—with one exception, in 1933, when, for a special occasion, I wrote and read publicly a kind of rather extensive "declaration of love" to music. I tell you all this to stress that what I am doing here I do as an excursionist, an outsider, not as an amateur; for the amateur does not perform in public.

I do not make this statement as an apology or as a request for indulgence; neither do I make it from modesty. As a musician, my efforts must be absorbed chiefly by writing, performing and teaching music. The travelling concert performer lives a rather lazy life. Most of his time—particularly if he presents himself everywhere on earth, wherever a demand for musical performances exists—has to be spent on ships, trains and planes. In the intervals between his travels he carefully has to keep his physique and his nerves fit for his public appearances, which always constitute a responsibility. Furthermore, he has to satisfy the greediness of publicity, has to meet social obligations, to hear and advise colleagues, and so forth. The weeks or months during which he does not mount platforms are partly devoted to preparation for the concert season. The amount of time spent in preparation depends entirely upon the type of performer and upon the range of his repertoire. I have known musicians who were capable of working on their compositions and of giving a concert as well as lessons all on the same day, almost every day and all the year round, and who, miraculously, still found time to write and talk about music and to participate fully in all the pleasures arranged in their honor.

I personally do not belong to those versatile "ants" who, incidentally, are by no means the norm. Thus, since performances in public had the first claim on my activities (thanks to the desire of the initiators of my career), I had, as you can imagine, not very much time left for composition—which I love most —and for teaching—which I love much. Even were I more certain of the advantage and profit gained for music by articles, books and lectures about it, and were I better suited to, and more attracted by, such efforts than is the case, the spare time granted to me after all the work I have first to do certainly would not be sufficient to cultivate the literary field with the seriousness that is due it. I have much too much respect for it to approach it lightly.

The books (not very many) which I have been able to read during short vacations or otherwise are mostly, as you will understand, not books on music. My knowledge of data, theories, systems, and my familiarity with the private affairs of great musicians are therefore very incomplete. The purely musical activity, which is my sphere, is not research work, not scientific (though it is nonetheless orderly), and not theoretical. Service in this purely musical sphere neither requires a scholar nor makes one. What I can say about music is exclusively a result of sheer musical experience in both meanings—experience through continual experiences. It seems important to clarify this point, for one might otherwise ascribe to me a pretension to be or to become a professional lecturer. Though such pretension is surely alien to me, I welcome the opportunity—for a musician who gladly sticks to his proper boundaries —to relate, without method or dogmatism, some of my ideas on music and on conditions which surround music.

To return now to my main subject, music: many musicians are occupied in the production and exhibition of music outside the province of art. Such goods (or evils) can be produced and exhibited miserably as well as brilliantly and in all intermediate shades.

It is my conviction that every musician—not only the master but the poorest performer of the shabbiest music—must have musical talent. Has it ever been investigated, is it susceptible of research, whether a musician's vocation can be decided upon as mechanically, or brought about as accidentally, as I presume must be the case in some other occupations for which no special gift or skill is wanted? Is music ever chosen because it is a "job" like other jobs? I doubt it. Although many musicians, in all departments, after deciding to become professionals, often seem to behave as if music were nothing else to them but a source of income, I doubt whether the decision taken by or for them, is often caused by mere speculation or by mere chance. I think that music calls all musicians, amateurs as well as professionals, writers of music and friends of music. The gift for music signifies the call. I am in a dilemma as to where to place the strummer to whom I denied the qualification of an amateur. Is he also gifted and called? It will be necessary to fix arbitrarily a point below which, in our differentiated civilization, a quality cannot be acknowledged as a part of that civilization.

Whether persons trading in and on musicians and their products have an inner relation to music or whether they only do business with it, as they would with any other article of merchandise, is difficult to know. Both types probably exist.

Until not so long ago, almost all professional musicians (except those who exercised rather primitive functions) devoted themselves to all three musical activities: writing, performing and teaching. The unfortunate division into composer and performer started, I suppose, with the increased output of musical works, the expansion of public musical life and the growing demand for performances. Some musicians in the past also wrote about music. The very great ones did not do so until the nineteenth century. Before that time music had a more or less local circulation. It was supported by the church, the courts and courtiers, but not as yet by an anonymous public. In Protestant churches the congregation participated in choral singing, but only a few of them, I think, went further in music than that.

Tabulations, textbooks, compendiums, and dictionaries concerning the rapidly enlarged and complicated mass of musical material appeared constantly in succession; for the most part they were put together by musicians better suited for sifting than for creative work. However, in the nineteenth century the musical genius also participated in the public discussion of music, its substance and appearance. Schumann, Weber, Berlioz, Mendelssohn, Wagner and Liszt wrote about music. Much of this literature is of lasting value and interest. None of it is of the schoolmaster type, nor is it pure research work, didactic or theoretical. They reviewed —in very friendly fashion—compositions and performances; they propagated idealism and suggested problems; they accelerated the organization of expanding musical education and the diffusion of music by practical, though not commercial, advice. Berlioz wrote an unsurpassed treatise on instrumentation, as well as a very human and moving volume of memoirs and other literary works. Only Wagner wrote polemically and in his own behalf.

The text books and pieces of music designed to develop such aptitudes as are demanded by masterpieces, increased enormously. The same was true of the more and more fashionable types of pieces which were intended as a sort of playground for exhibiting technical feats. Musical study material was provided by minor, yet remarkable talents; much of it is still in use and justifiably so. At approximately the same time, musicians began, often with great difficulty, to collect and compare all traceable versions of the works of their great predecessors. Academies of music, then established, proved very helpful to these endeavors.

The second half of the nineteenth century saw a remarkable lull in the literary activities of musicians; the greatest musicians of that period kept silent, presumably because specialists appeared to take over this branch of enlightenment. These specialists, (nonmusicians, if you accept my distinction), were those who studiously investigated and cleared the unexplored forest of musical production and musical life. Incidentally, chairs of music and lectures on music constitute one of the latest additions to musical institutions. In our age, composers (especially the most highly reputed exponents of the so-called new music) again participate in literary reflections on music. A parallel might be drawn with the musical situation in the first half of the nineteenth century which teemed with innovations. In contrast, however, with their colleagues of that day, our contemporaries indulge in theory. It may be that the innovations now, as they claim, are more far-reaching and fundamental than those which any other period has ever witnessed. Most of their writings and public talks about music are rather dogmatic pleadings for their own technical methods. This is new, for theories abstracted from newly invented technical devices in composition have, in the past, scarcely ever been presented by the inventors themselves.

I have arrived at the point where I must deal with the group of professionals who contribute to music by means of words only. Amateurs have no place in this group. Nearest to the musician in the group is the musical editor, the man who devises methods and provides solutions of technical problems, aids to musical production in general and in particular; the man who compiles, compares and contrasts, for musicians, the more important suggestions, while justly disregarding the astonishing amount of abstruse and fantastic speculation which flourishes in this particular field; the man who revises, edits, and comments upon musical works. That type of work will mostly be in the hands of people who actually practise music in one way or another.

Between them and those who render the accounts of the vast world of music, of its rise, its ways and its effects, stands the critic. The music critic is nowadays generally, almost automatically, understood to be a journalist. The use of criticism in journalism is a degeneration of criticism. Originally, criticism meant exposition, examination and discernment of ideas, of new ideas, either derived from older ones or contradicting them. Its sole purpose was to analyze the different modes of approach to knowledge and to solve the problems. This was done by the most learned and for the most learned persons, divided, of course, into polemical groups. Before we had compulsory education, all those who knew how to read and write were learned. Today, when everyone can read and write, one has to know first what it is that a person is reading, before one can class him among the still small minority of the learned, educated or cultured.

It is not for me to tell you how social development led to daily newspapers. The very term journalism seems here and there to be no longer the right one and could be better replaced by "minutism," since in the big cities all day long fresh newspapers are distributed at very brief intervals. And, to tell the truth, a considerable part of what is alleged to be news would perhaps in former times scarcely have been recognized as such.

The music critics of today, writing for the newspapers, have the established function of informing the "public" as to the qualities of musical works and performances whenever these are offered in public. Their criticisms are obviously not meant to instruct the musicians who are criticized or even to be read by them—although often the musicians could learn something from reports about concerts. Such an influence—on the musician and not merely on the public—might increase the importance of the critic for the production of music.

Remarks about music that arouse the attention and stimulate the thoughts of musicians do not come from critics alone. Some quite naive statement by a simple layman might be striking enough to alter some of the ideas of a musician. In this way it might have gained, quite unwittingly, a certain importance for music. But critics are not supposed to be naive; their connection with music and their importance to music does not proceed from the fact that musicians are occasionally influenced and helped by reviews. The majority of critics are professional musicians (preponderantly teachers) and are, therefore, connected with music in the most legitimate manner. However, in the biggest cities where so many concerts have to be reviewed, a critic is usually prevented from exercising a professional musician's activity. He will have barely as much time as an amateur, and will presumably have much less gusto. The critic is likely to be fed up with music, while the amateur is thirsty for it. What they have in common is the highly placed starting point and the upward direction.

As a rule, only music which can be classed as art is performed at concerts (though the rule is becoming dangerously loose), and only concert and opera performances—a very small portion of the music supply that is flooding our defenseless ears—are reviewed. Recently also records, whatever their musical level. To have to listen day after day for many months of the year to public performances, with the obligation to write about each of them, is no enviable lot. The same pieces and performers will appear on many different occasions. Two-thirds, at least, of all interpretations are bound to be mediocre, if measured by the highest standards. As for the music itself, the standard works of the past (selected by the great critic, time) are no longer subject to debate. A large percentage of contemporary works not yet tested by time immediately reveal their comparative feebleness, as has always been the case. But, after all, nobody is obliged to be a genius.

The critic is always an idealist, and for one who pursues musical—artistic—ideals, to be placed in journalism must cause him some uneasiness. Frequently it must occasion inner conflict. For what is characteristic of the newspaper is its indifference to quality. Good, mediocre and bad are quite mechanically juxtaposed in each edition. Love and business are not congenial mates. Nevertheless, considering the limited number of readers interested in artistic matters, the space allotted to such matters is rather extravagant. I have observed that this is true of many leading papers, and it occurs practically every day. To fill this space under all circumstances must present difficulties. What happens musically, in public, ranges from the sublime to the ridiculous, and all the way from high eminence to insufficiency. After the rare favor of a profound artistic experience nobody can wish to rush to a typewriter and reduce his exalted mood to words. Forced to do so, nobody can wish to see, the morning after, what he wrote under the spell of deep emotion and concentration, surrounded by columns of disinterested chatter. Every conscientious critic would wish again and again to return to the event which so affected him as to create a new outlook; but lack of space will prevent him from coming repeatedly back to it. On the other hand, no critic will wish, after an exhibition of hopeless self-deception, to attack the pitiable culprit (who did his best) with more than an embarrassing question; but this time, also, the available space may have to be filled.

I have mentioned extreme cases; the majority of performances will be about halfway between, and fairly similar to each other. Lack of vitality, eloquence and plasticity tend to assimilate uninspired accomplishments, irrespective of the school from which the tedium emanates. To think that the critic must evaluate each single fighter in the musical army—recruits as well as field marshals; glowworms as well as stars; the blessed, the just passable and the inept—one after the other—always filling *the same space!* Such a duty must, in many cases at least, constitute an act of self-denial. There is also the compulsion to be present at performances in conditions of fatigue, depression, or even occasional and quite understandable rebellion. No wonder that some critics, after decades of service, arrive at queer ideas about music. Their ambitions were focused on music, on fundamentals, principles, ideas and ideals; on lasting substances, the superpersonal and superprovincial—their practice had to deal with musicians, idols, persons; with ephemeral and external features; with petty details, antics, technicalities, data, applause and other trifles; and they found themselves obliged to write in a language not too austere for those who glance fleetingly at a newspaper page. Even all the musicians together and all they produce do not make up the whole of music. Music remains inexhaustible. The essence of music might, however, become obscured rather than revealed, if presented in excessive quantity, as in a metropolitan musical season.

Besides the danger of becoming blasé or cynical, there is—for the courted critic—the temptation to lose his modesty. Critics get tired, let me say, of the *Eroica* and don't mind saying so; forgetting that while they had the opportunity—nay, the obligation—to hear it dozens of times, the other listeners hear it only rarely; forgetting that every year there are many newcomers in the audience; forgetting also that musicians can never cease to use as test pieces such works as will always remain better than any conceivable performances of them. A critic, in short, might forget that neither the musician nor the public is placed as is he, the critic, the middleman between them—a human being, nevertheless, with innate or acquired idiosyncrasies.

I have already referred to these idiosyncrasies. They are sometimes expressed in propaganda for the obscure and the recherché; sometimes in a campaign for the plain and vulgar. After reaching the saturation point, critics are apt to decry the nobler intentions as intellectual affectation. Is it conceivable to enjoy without reserve, to embrace freely, to be open to the direct entrance of happiness, if one is restrained by the knowledge that after drinking at the source, the source has to be praised or criticized for the guidance of others? I wish, for the critics' sake, that it might be easier to overcome such difficulties than I imagine it is.

The occupation of a critic is evidently an exacting one, as is that of the musician or that of the teacher. In any occupation requiring unusual gifts only a small number of persons have succeeded in satisfying more than a fair portion of this occupation's requirements. Only a small number succeed now and, I dare say, will succeed in the future. To satisfy all demands is clearly impossible. Complaints about this state must be directed to nature. The achievements of the outstanding few provide the standards by which the results of all the efforts made by the lesser ones are measured. Mediocrity is an extremely elevated status considering that not much is above, but very much below. The excesses of publicity and advertising have falsified the notion of "mediocrity" to such an extent that it is now generally understood to be an almost insulting term of reproach. Though I have used it several times, I have never done so in a deprecating sense.

Great men are as rare among the critics as they are among the musicians or any other group, but the consequences of not being great are not the same for critics as they are for musicians who appear in public. Only the musicians are publicly criticized. The public's blind worship of printer's ink bestows upon almost every journalist the importance and prestige which properly is due only the best. The authority which is automatically bestowed upon each of them, and their natural protection from public opposition (for controversy is not usual amongst journalists on art) produce a twofold injustice. Newspaper readers, in general, consider the critic omniscient; those whom he criticizes privately blame him for not being omniscient. It is no fault of his. If a man accepts the position of critic, he is obliged, and must be prepared, to criticize everything and everybody. If you and I believe in the critic's omniscience because he is criticizing everything and everybody—in other words, just doing his job, we are very thoughtless. No individual, of course, can be an embodied musical encyclopedia; each individual is limited, and all one expresses beyond the reportage of bare facts, is inevitably personal. These are truisms, but they are forgotten again and again, or evaded, or misinterpreted. The fact that imperfection is the inescapable fate of each human being does not, of course, mean that all human beings are imperfect in the same degree and kind.

Journalism in art, as I said, exists for the information of the layman interested in art. Information is undoubtedly given, but often the information is sharply opposed to other information on the same subject and occasion. A layman who reads a morning as well as an evening paper and looks in both for the reviews of concerts, often learns—as his only information—the truth that even in an age of standardization taste has not yet been made uniform. A layman who reads only one paper, and always the same one, may easily have the bad luck to be informed by a person who happens not to be a luminary in his profession. Well, what then is the importance and effect of journalism on art? A cross section of all reviews on music written over two decades would probably describe quite well the musical situation during that period. Critics can be right and can be wrong; one and the same man can sometimes be right and sometimes wrong. The history of music has an abundance of amazing examples of fame gained in spite of the critics' hostility and contempt, and of failures suffered in spite of the critics' ardent support.

One temporary effect of journalism on music is often evident. Praise to the skies by the majority of papers can promote debutant musicians to heroes. It often happens that critics, startled at first by some impressive quality of a new musical figure slowly cool off (they must not disavow themselves too rapidly) and, in the end, are permanently disappointed by the musician whom they first had crowned with laurels. A nimbus is tenacious and draws adulators. But, for a while, at least, the prematurely heralded musician remains a hero, and the hero naturally advertises only the favorable judgments, never circulates the adverse criticisms. No musician has ever included in his propaganda material the sceptical voices which are spared to none! It also happens that all the praise in the world does not suffice to make a musician a hero if what he presents and represents is more exclusive than big audiences like; and there is no hero without big audiences. Occasionally forces stronger than the press—tradition, inertia, ladies' committees, managers—succeed in keeping at the top musicians whom the press denies the qualification to be there.

Much of what I have said about critics creating heroes or otherwise does not apply to the critics in smaller towns, especially where visiting musicians are concerned; for their reputation depends chiefly on the metropolitan press. This particularly explains why every musician who dreams of a public career thinks it indispensable to get examined and hallmarked in the metropolis. It is somehow tragicomical that public performances assume this air of school examinations, even in the case of accepted masterworks and mature, acknowledged masters. To calculate what efforts, of all mankind, were accumulated to reach a summit in Beethoven's *Missa Solemnis*, and what labor of generations was necessary, in order to produce a good performance of it; then to weigh that against what it might cost some very young man or girl to write twenty or more crushing lines about both—this might really lead to some mental discomfort. Yet Beethoven will not be dethroned, nor will his judges be dismissed. The sword of Damocles, in the shape of a press notice, hanging above each public performance, is not the driving power for the performer's desire to do his best. To eliminate possible error, let me say that composers and performers make their best efforts, not in order to please an audience and to get good reviews, but because the music within and without demands and commands it!

To sum up: press reviews about publicly performed music are intended to inform the audience, but not all of its members read them. They are not meant to teach musicians. Some of the readers of this intended information may dislike what is highly recommended, feeling superior or inferior to it. What, I ask once more, is the effect on music? Useful? Harmful? None? Even if only rarely useful, the institution would be justified. It is, in any case, obviously a necessity because of the way public life is being conducted, concert life organized, and musical traffic regulated. The critic is a musician and an idealist. He never wants to damage persons. He is obliged to adjust his work to inadequate environments. The best among the critics must arrive at a vexing dilemma: namely, to realize that what is objectionable to him, who is gifted and learned, who measures according to his ideals and his knowledge of the task, is yet very good and capable of revealing to an understanding audience some authentic beauties of musical art. What shall he write? He cannot say that it is good enough for them but not for him. Such a dilemma must ultimately lead to a compromise, in the interest of music, to call the good the best. This is a concession to the surprising claim that the "people" must always be given the best, though it is more than doubtful whether the best can even be perceived except by the few.

The scale of artistic merits differs for each individual. No authority is conceivable which could alter this natural dispensation—not even a dictator! Despite the strong present tendencies towards nihilism among intellectuals, these varying reactions to artistic values, and consequently different opinions concerning them, have not yet led to a denial of (distinctions between) artistic values. This is due, I think, to normal man's inclination to consider what he likes as superior to what he likes less. We may suppose that everybody—every normal person, I repeat—has preferences. Such discrimination, unless it is checked, must, of course, produce anarchy. To be fair, very many persons, if they are not pleased with a certain piece of music, say, and believe, that they are not pleased only because they do not "understand" it. What this confession actually means is never quite clear to a musician. At any rate, he has his misgivings about it.

To mitigate the confusion, efforts have been devoted since ancient times to the detection of the criteria by which an absolutely valid hierarchy of artistic values could be established. For music as an art—the youngest of the arts—such attempts began not very long ago, but they became so attractive that more and more minds became occupied with the problems. These minds, too, contribute to music only by means of words. The importance of their work is to be seen in the accurate inspection and scholarly interpretation of the gradual refinement of music and its development into an independent, ample complex, a priceless and inseparable part of our civilization's noblest and truest resources.

Pure musicians rarely participate in these activities—activities which require a scientific type of talent and, in any case, take much time. I have said before that the musicologist who possesses the qualities of historian, philosopher in esthetics, analyst and sociologist, probably chooses music as his subject of research because he loves music. He is probably active in it, and has certainly practised it already as a child. Systematic study of all the ingredients constituting music is a preparatory stage for research, and the enormous quantity of music and data usually known to musicologists continually astonishes the musician, making him almost ashamed of his own limited knowledge. But to be both the living raw material of music and its dissector is too great an ambition.

All the investigations and speculations of the musicologist have not succeeded in establishing absolute standards for building a doctrine devoid of ambiguity. They may even increase the existing confusion produced by the different effects of music on different listeners; these latter may now read books on music presenting different suggestions for this insoluble problem—how to define as a magnitude what can only be received and appreciated by individual impressions. I shall come back to this irritating point. The most intelligent, penetrating and original of such books are intellectually exacting and, therefore, are not widely circulated. There is greater demand, on the other hand, for popular, short, showy, sentimental and dramatic biographies of great or fashionable musicians, and also for a type of information about music which corresponds to that in guide books for sightseeing tourists. There is also a demand for stories and statistics which more or less deliberately pander to poorer taste. These are usually dressed up as propaganda for ideals.

All this literature, however, distracts one from the real issues. Annotations to programs are also of very questionable value. Musical periodicals or magazines, with the exception of those given over to the serious discussions of ideas and conditions, are for the most part mere advertisement plantations interspersed with articles and gossip. There are also reviews and criticisms, but these are merely fillers. They cannot be classified together with journalistic writing on musical art. Something quite different is intended. What they admittedly want is just advertisements which, remarkably enough, they get, though these mean nothing—at least nothing for music—and probably little for the prosperity of musicians.

Lectures on music are divided practically in the same manner as literature on music—exploration and exploitation of music. Encyclopedias of music also have existed, since the eighteenth century, and they are periodically supplemented with the necessary augmentations. Some are carefully arranged by conscientious scholars and are indispensable for cultured people as books of comprehensive reference; some are very careless imitations of the good examples and, therefore, only a nuisance.

What is the real issue? Simply music? The spirit, the generator of music, a phenomenon sending to man's mind tones, an imagination of sounds, urging him to release them to a boundless variety of incorporeal structures called compositions which need a transformation into material sounds—performances—to reach their final destination and reality? Or, is the final destination reached only when the material sounds return through the senses of one listening to his mind, and through it, back to its unknown origin—the divine reality? Well, we human beings have been given a wondrous present, a primary source of happiness, which is felt, whether we express ourselves by using it, or have our emotions aroused by hearing a performance by someone else.

Music cannot hurt. Sunshine can burn you, food can poison you, words can condemn you, pictures can insult you; music cannot punish—only bless. Now, what have we done with it—done with it since we recognized it as specifically musical language distinct from sounds as words? Roughly generalizing, we know three modes of application of music—all three still employed today; one among primitive groups of men, one among groups with a grand cultural past, and the third, our own, still in motion, which has seemingly very little in common with the other two. Only our Christian European civilization has been inspired to individuate music, to dispense it in a multitude of different forms, to raise it to a state of full sovereignty. Neither in the first nor in the second group does man seem to have divined the potentialities of music or felt an impulse to move on after a few initial steps. I have not heard of any group of men now alive, which lives entirely without music, without tones, arranged and exercised consciously. Physically, man can exist without music;

thus the presence of music among them must satisfy some instinct other than a physical desire.

The primitive groups, the so-called savages, developed their social institutions to a relatively innocuous degree, from which they, since we have had an opportunity to watch them, neither ascended nor descended. They have no classes in our sense; no aristocracy, bourgeoisie or proletariat, though undoubtedly by a certain distribution of labor they assigned different functions to men, women and elders. But they all live under equal conditions—the chieftains only in somewhat larger huts. Their rituals are as fixed as their entertainments. I think that under such conditions it is justifiable to consider all symbolical expressions of fear, hope, joy and sorrow as art, for no one in such a group knows of other than the accepted symbols, which are established once for all, nor does he wish for others. And where no discrimination can be applied, no clue exists for a distinction between values.

These primitives progressed to the limits of their creative capacity, which probably corresponded to their desire. The height they reached is accessible, the few patterns which they invented for their religious and other performances are comprehensible and valid for each of them. Their music is always auxiliary; it is never polyphonic; it is executed by singing, the only other instrument used being the simplest type of drum. The arrangement of tones (which, by the way, is a handy technical definition

You all know of the glorious unfolding of human creative genius in antiquity. The accomplishments of the oriental communities in those ancient times have never been surpassed—I would even say have never been equalled—in later times. We ought not to forget that they were the founders of what we understand to be civilization. This is not intended to belittle the grandiose attainments of human beings who, from obscure beginnings via the cave man, advanced to the apparently stabilized level of aborigines as we know them. Which of the human developments covers the greatest distance—the progress of man's primeval condition to the cave man's organization, from there to the present-day aborigines, from aboriginal art to the creations of the orient, or from oriental art to the shape of things today? I cannot imagine what it must have been to progress to the first stage; but I know that it is pretty difficult to progress now, with the immense quantity of ideas and material, much of which seems quite unnecessary, but which is being forced upon us, and at an almost paralyzingly rapid speed.

The creative eras of the orient and of the Mediterranean area in classical times provided ample work, copious satisfaction and even conflict for man's soul, his senses and his intellect. The results were equally great in the rational and irrational, the material and spiritual sphere. I need not go into detail about the innumerable emanations of man's genius, his supreme, comprehensive capacity in that great age.

But why was music almost static in Egypt, Persia, China; among the Jews and among the Moors; in Greece and Rome, and in other countries partaking of these cultures? Why was it treated as though it were not destined to major transformation and development? There was no limit—no sign of fatigue—in the fecundity of these ages, as manifested in the ennoblement of religion, poetry, drama, philosophy, science, architecture and other inspired expressions and adornments—and amusements as well. But in contrast to the other applicable mediums of artistic production, music did not evolve to much greater differentiation than the patterns known to primitives. It remained an auxiliary or accompaniment to extra-musical acts and events, an animation or allayment. Music in oriental culture (and I take the liberty of adding to it also Greek and Roman culture) seems to have been enriched only in proportion to the increase in the situations it was chosen to serve. Some refinements surely resulted from the increasing variety of services; more man-made instruments came into use; there may have been a gradual development of the ambition to adjust music to a particular atmosphere, delicate and private, solemn and festive, or robust and mobbish. For new groups arose within the group, and the time was gone when everything could be done or enjoyed by everybody. Discrimination must inevitably have followed.

I presume that even music, though it did not proceed very far, began to be divided into several quite definite talent, privileged by being one-sided, so to say, has not even a choice within the general choice. He must follow the summons. He and his work are bound to be distinguished from what others, not as definitely summoned, or summoned to another goal, are and do.

Discrimination is accepted as a basis of valuation. Nature distributes the gifts which men value—distinguishing between productive and receptive capacities. There are talents common to all, some common to many, and some common only to a few individuals. It is obvious that even the greatest creative genius, if physically normal, could succeed in doing the very important job, for example, of a scavenger. But it is surely a wise act of providence to have charged only a few with the duty of representing genius for all the others, for otherwise, the countless number of hands and brains of menials—with many functions below the king's majestic office—which are required for the indispensable services of our complex human organization might not be available. The machine has made many of them temporarily superfluous, but we cannot expect, in consequence, that providence in the future might shift to the production of more geniuses. If we could, it would be a comfort, since they are provided by nature and under all circumstances with a fully absorbing task; so they would at least never run the risk of being out of work.

Discrimination could be dismissed if everybody—or nobody—could be a genius. I don't think that either of these totalitarian chances is threatening us seriously. We shall, for a while, still be obliged to discriminate.

In conclusion, I wish to quote to you three aphorisms—all three of which will, I consider, help to illuminate the problem of discrimination. The first is by Goethe: "What is the universal? The unique phenomenon! What is the particular? An everyday occurrence!" This is a rather free translation of the original version, which reads: "*Was ist das Allgemeine? Der einzelne Fall! Was ist das Besondere? Millionen Fälle!*"

The second is by Lichtenberg, a German eighteenth century mathematician and philosopher. He was blamed for being too discriminating—critical to the point of arrogance. He protested by saying that he had noticed that the title of genius is given to man by other men, just as the caterpillar got the name "centipede," only because people are too lazy to count to fourteen. Since this discovery of his, he said, he could not accept any figure before examining it thoroughly himself. And, finally, there is the moving sentence by Maury: "Proud if I compare myself; humble if I consider myself," In the original, "*fier quand je me compare; humble quand je me considère.*"

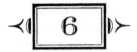

Music, as I have pointed out, was not benefited to any considerable extent by the creation and expansion of cultural values which occurred during that extravagantly fertile period before Christianity and Europe took the lead. Within the institutions of the primitive peoples music qualified as an art. Being not less developed than any other exalted symbolical expression, though represented only in a few slightly different patterns, it possessed the essential requirements of art. Within the great civilizations of the ancient orient and the Mediterranean, the germs of arts other than music grew to organisms of lasting importance and influence. Therefore, music, which was kept in an inferior position, does not belong to the art treasure of these civilizations. It was one of a group of conveniences devised to lend additional color or flavor, or sometimes, at opportune moments, a background to particular situations.

Art is not convenience, is not just *one* feature of some structure; it is an independent organism and each single representation of it is independent as well. It is its intrinsic nature to be released by the noblest aspiration of man and addressed to the noblest aspiration of man, to be released by man's profoundest demands on himself, by his conscious desire for contact with invisible reality and unequivocal truth—in a region that is above the egotistical, the utilitarian and the mechanical. There is no evidence of anyone's having experienced essential contact with art, unless his experience has both started and arrived at this—which constitutes the loftiest impulse, the richest awareness of man; unless the same experience determines his attitude towards other and less idealistic impulses and necessities; and unless it blesses him with that unassailable serenity which willingly accepts struggle, conflict, sorrow and imperfection as a price to be paid for the privilege of inseparable relation to it. Art is not an occasional refuge or a holiday, but a perpetual and inexhaustible mandate to our spirit. The efforts to fulfill this mandate belong to the most exacting, most satisfying, and therefore, to the supreme functions of man.

I know quite well how rigid is this interpretation of art, and how far distant from the indulgent and all too catholic conception almost generally welcomed, that no obligation is included in love of art. Art belongs to the world of love, which, of course, also commands other forces to fulfill the longing for completion—not absorption. Needless to say, art is neither the only workshop for human creative genius nor the only source of stimulation for thought and imagination, or of pleasure and excitement. But love, in all its creations, remains the most inspiring power in man's life, connecting him always with the transcendental, and with eternal problems. We call beautiful all that touches and moves the cherished loving side within us, but only he who moves can be moved.

Music has an exceptional, an incommensurable position among the arts. It is movement and, therefore, always future—never to be grasped. It is incapable of description; it has no practical use; one can—and can best—experience it without any extra-musical association. One can, of course, "associate"; and many who do associate at all associate the same piece of absolute music now with one, now with another abstraction. Program music is, therefore, essentially, a delusion.

The greater a musical work of art, the more will it include of the total expressive potency of music. This fact explains why persons related to music by grace, contemplate, perform and hear a work familiar to them at the next stage of their development as a work in many respects different from what they believed it to be before. This, I repeat, applies only to the real masterworks. The lesser works do not change as much, which explains why we, once liking them, at another stage of our development don't like them any more. It is an axiom that the greater includes the lesser. Therefore, the greatest works of music include all types, even the cheapest. But this constitutes such a tiny element in the all-inclusive great work that nobody notices its presence there. When we hear a noble and serious work of lesser inspiration, we often recognize a spiritual affinity (though not an actual reminiscence) to the greatest. This is always a credit to the composer, for it indicates that something of the spirit of the master lives in his work.

It is actually the same with performances. The true manner of interpreting one of the greatest works will invariably also be suited for the rendition of any very good work. It will comprise all the elements of any musical performance. How thoughtless it is to presume that a musician capable of attempting, with some satisfactory result, the reproduction of a consummate masterpiece might be incapable of succeeding with lesser works. He can, of course, without any effort execute any work below his major capacity, but music itself will occasionally forbid a musician to descend from the level to which it has assigned him. If, nevertheless, he tries to leave this level, he may fail on the lower level because he cannot be quite honest in a task that does not require all his qualities. Deeply honored, he will accept the kind of limitation which keeps him exclusively in those upper regions where the summits continually seem to rise and rise, no matter what height one has attained; and in his innermost being he will feel the obligation to follow a direction which leads him to the worthiest of all struggles—the struggle for moderation along the line of *most* resistance.

Pessimistic disbelief in the force of things as they are, whether as a pretext, an escape, or a kind of relief, has no validity. The imposed limitation might narrow the radius of an artist's work to the cultivation of a few sections only of the rich soil where great musical art flourishes. His full talent, his life perhaps, will be demanded for the conquest of the assigned sector; and before he has achieved it, even the strongest attraction cannot divert him to another—perhaps equally exalted—sector of the art. Yet, an artist's capacity to produce, perform or teach great music is a pass key to all parts belonging to it; it enables him (it cannot be said often enough) under all circumstances to excel in any lower type as well. He shuns it only because he has got something better to do. (Incidentally, the unfortunate distinction between "Classicism" and "Romanticism" should be abolished. The process of artistic creation is always the same—from inwardness to lucidity.)

A performer in the group of—let me call them— the communicators of the interior of deeply inspired music is often praised for a supposed self-effacement, for the suppression of his personality, for the eschewing of sensational features—all of which he had never had in mind. What a mistake, arrived at by an entirely negative reflection! The absence of certain elements which may be quite legitimate in another (perhaps more pleasurable) branch of music is no sign of unselfishness or subordination, but just evidence of a normal sense of locality. It is not particularly flattering to a so-called personality to hear that he or she "appears" on the lower levels but disappears on the "heights." A performing artist should be in the position of a mountain guide. A guide's

and concessions they have to make, about conde-
scension, catering to the "gallery," the "man in the
street" and the "tired businessman" (two mythical
beings) is fallacy. The writer of the most successful
popular tune of the day has climbed as far up as it
was given to him to climb, even if he thinks himself
to be actually a writer of oratorios (a type of music
in which, unfortunately, there is no cash), and has
deliberately degraded himself to do "what the
people like." All musicians do their best; the quality
of talent decides their *choice* of music; the quantity of
talent decides the *effect*. One can neither become a
genius nor a moron by volition.

Recital programs in our concert routine, in most
cases, are a mixed list of items of admittedly unequal
qualities. Such programs are arranged like a foreign
visitor's day in Paris—from cathedral to night club;
in other words, from the highest downward. The
normal route of idealistic ambitions begins high and
continues upward. The programs of chamber music
ensembles and orchestras are not as a rule as vari-
able and extensive; they are better balanced, more
homogeneous and therefore more highly respected
than the "popular" education-pleasure-fashion
pattern. But even the orchestras today (since the

conductor has, following the path of the singer and the instrumentalist, become the concert hall's latest prima donna) show a dubious inclination toward the potpourri style of program. The heroes of the *solo* recital indulge, almost without exception, in this style. The virtuoso, the star (a paradoxical title for persons who produce chiefly fireworks), is equally at home in the upper and the lower regions, and sincere in both. But sincerity and seriousness, although they must be assumed to exist in an artist, are not in themselves productive qualities. They are not identical with talent and should, without ado, always be taken for granted.

The term "virtuoso" is today a misnomer. Originally, as is obvious from its etymology, it did not mean what it means today. It referred to the subject, not the treatment. The *what* and not the *how* determined the title. The what belonged invariably to the upper regions. The present conception is misleading because it implies—at least suggests—a distinction between him who adapts music to *his* most efficient qualities and the type of performer who serves the demands of *music*. (The first virtuoso in this modern sense was Procrustes, who stretched the short and cut the long pieces.) It is generally believed that of the two types the so-called virtuoso needs the greater technical equipment. A ridiculous idea! All masterworks demand the total of all imaginable technique, but only in a secondary function. In so-called virtuoso pieces the means are also the end. Masterworks demand the communication of the interior, whence they originate; the virtuoso pieces are on the other hand, mostly façades. Since they contain comparatively little music, not much more than technique is required for even adequate performance. But works which are music in every tone cannot be communicated if not much more than technique is at the disposal of the performer. Under such circumstances, everyone feels in a mysterious way that the essential is lacking; for here technique itself misses the effect which it always arouses if applied to pieces that are chiefly dedicated to technique.

It ought to be clear, then, that the virtuoso type of music is the less exacting type, both for performer and listener. It is less exacting for the listener, because the accomplishments are measurable, the alleged risks tangible, and because the listener's excitement is physical. Coloratura, swing and acrobatics provide similar sensations. Jazz bands have a vertiginous "virtuosity." Liszt's rhapsodies are mostly well performed; Mozart's symphonies scarcely ever.

Great music is often criticized for not being well written for the instrument. But a piece of music is well written for the instrument if the piece comes to full expression only, or at least best, on that particular instrument. It is known that comparatively inferior musical works can be effectively presented also on instruments other than those for which they were written; some even might, without suffering serious damage, be transcribed for barrel organs. The greater part of Beethoven's piano music, on the other hand, can be communicated only by means of the piano, which proves that Beethoven knew how to write for it.

The objections to his and other masters' treatment of the piano, violin, voice, orchestra, etc., are in truth criticisms of the music. The common belief that the employment of brilliant passages and other devices for the display of technical tricks proves a composer's understanding of the instrument is erroneous. If it were true, it would mean that Schubert did not write as well for the human voice as did Arditi.

Furthermore, I do not believe that great composers are ever inspired by the specific qualities of instruments. In compositions employing several different instruments the same musical phrases are given to many of them—now as a solo, now in a combination, now in unison. I believe that the conception of musical ideas in the composer's mind is followed by a gradual inner indication· as to which of the available instruments might best be suited to convey these ideas.

The instrument chosen by the composer must therefore be accepted as an ideal one, the best imaginable in its category. A composer who has an old and defective upright piano does not write his piano piece for his particular poor example of a piano, and if he writes a song he certainly desires a fine voice to perform it.

The compositions of Bach, Mozart, Beethoven, Schubert, and other creators of great music often contain parts of exceptional audacity, of profound and everlasting independence, parts which can neither be related to rules nor serve to establish rules. Such parts, beyond convention and tradition, impose new and superior demands upon performers and often also upon instruments. Many musicians, now and in the past, feel uneasy with such elements in music—elements which apparently resist domestication. Special qualities are required to enjoy and love and absorb these "wild" elements. Musicians without these special qualities, not knowing or not admitting their limitations, are inclined to consider these portions to be "misfits," caused by errors in writing, incompleteness of notation, defective theoretical knowledge, physical disturbances (such as deafness), etc., etc. Judgments of that sort are too naive to be discussed; alterations based on such judgments are unpardonable.

The "technique exhibitors" have a comparatively small repertoire, because part of the literature suitable for them is "dated," while part of it is unpresentable. Thus they all play practically the same pieces, in a competitive tendency that is alien to music but proper for technique. The other types of performer, the "music transmitters," differ much more in their repertoire, having the advantage of feeding from a great wealth of lasting values. Their tendency is not competitive, but cooperative.

To correct the misconception concerning "virtuosity," which (I must emphasize once more) must also be completely mastered for the performance of inwardly originated music, although it is generally related to the external (which is about all there is to the other species), Walter J. Turner, the English poet, has suggested giving to the so-called "virtuoso" a new name. The name is "trashoso"—which would precisely express what is nowadays expected from the virtuoso.

The virtuosos who perform both types of music— both often very well though rarely equally well— are not considered virtuosos by their audiences so long as they devote themselves to the heart-stirring part of their occupations. As for many of the virtuosos, whose critical sense and probably atavistic conscience do perhaps not quite approve of what their instinct and talent urge them to produce, who, in short, do not like to like what they like—burden the public (that most welcome silent scapegoat) with the responsibility for that collision, and for their own deviation from acknowledged ideals. A really great artist once complained to me that to smuggle Beethoven into the masses one has to wrap his music up in Lehar's. Whether he believed it or not, it is objectively untrue, and moreover, will never work. Who presents treasures *and* trash cannot claim to be a champion for the treasures, for he always takes the risk that the trash might be preferred. The famous sentence that "the end justifies the means" plainly refers to rotten means, otherwise it would be absolutely superfluous. It is similar to the slogan "Keep Smiling." It invites one to smile where normally one would, and should, grumble.

It surely is no shame for an artist to be versatile; to find genuine pleasure in mere virtuosity, which can be most ingenious and vital. Yet a man of standing should not excuse himself for actions which he could omit without any loss to his prestige and welfare. Nobody can believe that an artist who has arrived at the top in regard to public appreciation is obliged to sacrifice himself to help his career. If he wishes to act on different levels, he should openly declare that he is acting as he wishes. It would be better taste and probably more correct to say that when he plays good music he is making an excursion upwards, than to say that when he plays cheap music he is making concessions downwards, which, to begin with, nobody had asked him to do. He does not sacrifice himself; he does not hate himself and what he is doing, and there is no reason whatsoever why he should. He is simply many-sided, though occasionally he might long to be one-sided.

With young and not yet publicly very successful artists, it is different. They may be torn in two directions, pressed by teachers, friends and family, bewildered by artistic conditions, seduced by popular standards, driven by economic hardships, and so forth. For a long time they may really not know where to go. The line of least resistance is so alluring.

And that brings me back to the subject of promiscuous programs. A common objection to programs which include only works of that artistic quality which is generally recognized as the best, is that they are not composed like good menus. I have heard this innumerable times, but the simile seemed to me just as false and stupid the first time as the last. Why expect a concert program to correspond to a good menu at all? And by the way, not a great many members of concert audiences can be suspected of enjoying a good menu very often. But let us, for a joke, examine the comparison. A good menu opens with hors d'oeuvres, appetizers—an equivalent, I should think, to encores at a concert, where, curiously enough, they are always served at the end. (Encores, by the way, originate in the old custom of paying for applause.)

The menu proper comprises soup, fish, poultry, well-cooked vegetables—which, especially in a good menu, are all very light and digestible food. But the "serious" music which fills the first half of recitals is always called heavy meat, apparently a kind of medieval peasant feast! The desserts in a good menu— puddings, much cream, *crepe* (often prepared with alcohol)—are hardly light or digestible. Yet the "light" music (the entertainment after the duty) is considered to represent the sweets of the menu. And the drinks that accompany a good meal are apt to get stronger and stronger from course to course, certainly in France, where they really understand these things.

In any case, the first condition of a good menu is that all dishes should be prepared by the same chef or several chefs of equal merit; that all should be prepared with first-class raw materials, and that the gourmet should concentrate with the same seriousness on all of them. Just the opposite applies to the usual music menu. It is like a stroll from an expensive place to cheaper and cheaper places, with the idea that the patron must be compensated for the hard demands made on his palate at the better place, by a more comfortable treatment at the inferior one. What is actually advocated by that unfortunate simile is perfectly realized by a program containing exclusively music of one quality, namely the best. A symphony, a sonata or string quartet provide the desired contrasts in their different movements. The artist who performs only good music chooses the single items of his program very carefully, paying special attention to the greatest possible diversity, which in any case is an artistic demand. In this he meets with no difficulties, for the treasure of masterworks at his disposal provides an endless range of selection from the strict to the playful, and permits a complete display of all the virtues conceivable in a performer. But always it remains *one* quality. I wish to emphasize here that the opposite to "serious" is not "light," but "unserious!" And programs, which are not the usual melange, which exclude the cheap, also indicate a better opinion of the audience.

It is said again and again that music lovers must first be educated before they can be expected to enjoy only *good* concert music. This is maintained, although for generations concerts have been given by most celebrated musicians. And yet we still wait. In fact, the programs on the average have become worse and worse. The great creative virtuoso of the nineteenth century—the legitimate favorite of the big audiences—is dying out. The result is a gap. His place in the market is being taken more and more by dancers. They invade and conquer the concert platform, using sovereign and austere music as a servant, simply because one can dance or move to any music. Other entertainers from the spectacle department, who previously would never have pretended to such honor, are now also appearing in so-called concerts.

The theater, on the other hand, only rarely admits the hybrid program. The works given in the theater normally last too long to be performed two or more in succession. (The same is true of oratorios in music.) The operatic repertoire, however, contains more short works, and operas, therefore, occasionally present strange juxtapositions. Shows and circuses offer variegated amusements, but only amusements. They are thus far being kept clean. Who knows how soon we may be favored with a

Noel Coward-Shakespeare night, with both items, of course, cut down!

A specialty of the concert hall is the appearance of the aged performer who still executes the same feats which brought him triumphs when he was very young. This does not extend to singers, of course, on whom physiology sets a limit. Old actors play the parts of old persons. Sportsmen at a certain age stop their attempts to break records. Music is neither descriptive nor competitive. Nevertheless, one could easily define what kind of musical performance is not quite appropriate for people in full maturity (for instance, mere bravura).

Yet there is something in musical performances which permanently invites performers to exhibit dexterity. Brilliant effect is possible simply with speed or noise, or speed and noise. But since this kind of effect is fairly sure to be produced, while the effect produced by solutions of artistically nobler tasks is not so sure (unless the task is well solved), the preference of the safer line becomes quite understandable. This brings up that very strange confusion already mentioned, about the different degrees of difficulty of execution. Only that is really difficult, which cannot be learned, or at least which cannot be learned by incessant practising. There is no rivalry between perseverance (the capacity to sit, if it is a question of the piano) and genius (which is located elsewhere). A genius could scarcely be expected to spend hours and hours every day just in order to train his fingers and muscles. Also, that would be quite futile and superfluous, except for the satisfaction of athletic ambitions. No sportsman, by the way, trains after the fashion of a musical technician. The marathon runner does not start his daily training by first walking slowly for an hour, no tennis champion begins with high and soft shots. Musical performers have been intimidated by an error of instruction first committed in the nineteenth century, and which is still being committed now. To isolate the acquisition of technique from the subject which it will later have to serve is nonsense.

I shall now return for a short visit to the ancient world. What might have been the reason for the comparative sterility of music in the age of pre-Christian civilizations? To me the most plausible explanation is that the available means of satisfying the spiritual and emotional requirements of the times must have been sufficient. The gradual decadence of the Eastern creative energy, helping, perhaps evoking the gradual ascendancy of Christianity, must have metamorphosed man's internal and external existence. The corruption of secular forces, not impeded by their gods, made people ripe for a doctrine teaching salvation through inwardness and humility. Music is the right medium in which to express devotion to the spirit. Music is complete in every individual. It might, in those days, for the first time have been separated from any purpose, for the first time recognized as a comfort for a lone being and as an activity in itself, motivated by a desire to communicate to the silent universe emotion and imagination and purest expectancy. A joy in improvisation might have been aroused, after the disintegration of conventions, and music's higher destination and mission discovered.

Ever since that time this new personal relation to music has been cultivated without interruption. As it wandered westwards, where groups without recorded cultural past comparable to that of the East began to build on the foundations of eastern culture, Roman colonization and Nordic migration formed the link. Planned promotion of music towards its glorious future was first still the work of the East, of the Christian church in the Roman Empire of the East, which suffered its breakdown much later, and for a long time formed the center between Orient and Occident. The musical elements refined and organized there were, of course, taken from the extant patterns. All groups not converted to Christianity, some of them still splendidly productive during the Middle Ages, did not, to my knowledge, greatly alter the traditional function of music. Again, probably no inner necessity was felt to establish a personal contact with it or to gain independence for it. The type of religious creed could also explain the different attitude. The ancient Jews, the creators of monotheism, perhaps never enjoyed sufficiently stable conditions to further the arts. They were pioneers in the field of education and, with their firm individual bond with God, were possibly not in need of many symbols.

The eventual decline of Eastern Rome brought a neglect of cultural activities—music included. The charge of music remained in the hands of a rather small sector of the Christian church. The Orthodox branch of the church in Russia and the Balkans atrophied musically. The Irish monks contributed much to music's further development and circulation. Soon, in its now elevated state it resumed an auxiliary position in consequence of the turn and return to secular and social splendor. But the sacred and the profane types were now decidedly different, and the performance of both surely freer and much more individual than ever before. The refining and enriching preoccupation with music went on chiefly in monasteries where, I suppose, the individual composer was slowly bred. It is a justified conjecture that professionals, or at least semi-professionals, existed in the monasteries, in the church, amongst minstrels and bards, at country fairs; and also that there were chivalrous amateurs at the courts.

First experiments with the notation of music date from that period. The most decisive addition to music appeared with part-singing, which means the initiation of harmony, of "vertical" music. All this is commonplace enough, but I have to mention it because of its part in the transition to music's full independence and full stature as an art. As an art, music became the head of a big family of products, all labelled with the same name, but very heterogeneous in quality and tendency. It had become a symbolical, transcendental, condensed expression and the summit of an undulated landscape, an inexhaustible cup of delight and a permanent sphere of action for the individual. It is the incessant supply of personal work of a creative and idealistic nature, of a volume large enough to absorb the total working capacity of an extensive community of individuals, who make and elucidate music; and on the other hand the incessant supply of experience and pleasure to innumerable other individuals who receive music—it is all of this that signifies the absolutely new character of music's function.

The weight of man's conscience, postulated by the Christian doctrine, resulted in a sense of individual responsibility hitherto scarcely felt by him, and this new spiritual claim had to be satisfied by a strictly personal service, upwards, to the maker of conscience. The personal control of ethical and sentimental disturbances, the consciousness of duality (or plurality), consciousness of individual and social necessities and obligations—all in one and the same person—created requirements unknown before. These established and deepened our personal rela-

or learned. If we have not yet arrived at this almost paradise-like uniformity, education, mechanization, and business, it appears, will soon have us there. For the moment, to be sure, we are in a crisis and in some confusion. Many refer to our glorious past; many to our glorious future. Some say that music flourishes at present; some that it withers. Music also has become a big department store (symbol of our age) and, when talking about music, one should name the department he has in mind (if any), otherwise the term remains as vague as the term money, which applies equally to a penny and a billion.

Our age, a fortress of materialism, both Right and Left, is automatically in favor of quantities. Nature has not yet ceased to endow man with idealistic hunger, but it is not so easy to satisfy it within the walls of materialism. If he could live as destiny presumably intends him to do, between the poles of idealism and materialism, and could incline to the side that attracts him most, it would be easier. Our civilization, having lurched up to one of the two poles (materialism), apparently finds it difficult to keep the equilibrium. We have to adjust ourselves to a one-sided position. The quantity of music on the market is undoubtedly immense—an important member of commodities and utilities. If we consider that no motion picture house, dance hall or restaurant is without music, often produced by machines, that scarcely a single home, not a single shop is without a radio, that we can already rent apartments with music "on tap," it reaches the dimensions of a plague. In addition to the other pleasures that call us we can boast of a permanent avalanche of entertainment.

How much of that plethora of music partakes of the nature of art? Will all the people who are present where music is heard (I mean music that is not art) one day ask for art? Do all the people who listen to music that is art know that it is art? The answers to these questions, given by persons concerned with music, would not be unanimous. What the answers would be is irrelevant. The people like the one or the other type or several types of music, and they know which they like. But what is actually revealed by such a statement? The circulating quantity and quality of music has become a supply that precedes the demand, just as women's fashions in all branches precede the demand. Is there any recognizable plan, line, tendency in this supply? I wonder whether it is not altogether an industry, directed by a mentality which is paralyzed by always thinking of the many —a contagious effect of mass-production.

In earlier times, art was entrusted to the hands of a minority—a minority placed on an elevation in the center. Now it has been moved to Main Street where everything is exhibited. Is it the same as before? In most countries where musical culture meant very much to a group of individuals related to it by a strong inner demand, men have conducted and still conduct the artistic activities; in some countries it is the women. Can it be the same?

I was brought up in Vienna in the 'nineties, and was very fortunate as a boy in being at home in two musical circles: the one given to the timeless, the other to the more ephemeral; the one centering around Brahms, the other around Anton Rubinstein. At that time there worked in Vienna Brahms, Bruckner, Hugo Wolf, Johann Strauss, the young Gustav Mahler. Schoenberg was a rising star. I heard almost every day about those men from their friends. They all lived in very modest conditions, although Brahms, for instance, already enjoyed world fame. I remember distinctly that the first artist I ever heard mentioned in connection with business was Richard Strauss. Even when Sarasate, the violin virtuoso, or Adelina Patti, the prima donna, were talked about, the discussion was never concerned with their incomes or popularity. And Richard Strauss was only accused of exacting high fees from publishers, never of gathering information as to what the man in the street would like, in order that he might try to please him and so enlarge his clientele.

Then, as now, there were four types of music: popular music, salon music, virtuoso music, and music of a timeless tendency—only the latter being pure art, by the nature of that very tendency. Within the three lower types, particularly the "popular" one, what was and is produced often shows talent, vitality, charm and fire; within the fourth, much is boring and eclectic, and disappears rapidly. Though Johann Strauss wrote for his day, we are still delighted by his ever fresh creations. Longevity of a composition proves its unusual value but does not necessarily make it art. (Johann Strauss, by the way, would surely have protested against his pieces being performed on the same program with a Beethoven symphony.)

What decides the category in which a production belongs? It cannot be success or failure; it cannot be personal taste. The idea that two different things are equal because both are enjoyed by different persons or by one person, is utterly absurd. It seems impossible for people enjoying music to describe to each other exactly what they have received from it. There are no two people who receive exactly the same effect. To be pleased by some music or performance cannot mean that they are unsurpassable. Advertising, beyond the limit of mere announcement, is clearly not modesty and truthfulness, both qualities which are essential criteria of art. Art itself, of course, cannot advertise; nor is it always the artist himself who advertises. But advertised they are, and always as "outstanding." This must bewilder, mislead, and eventually alienate persons who have not enough self-confidence to ignore publicity, nor the right connections to gather advice from more reliable sources.

Now, briefly, a few important musical problems: To protect musical works from piracy, the nineteenth century inaugurated the copyright law, which, however, expires after a fixed time, subject in America to a limited renewal. Beyond that, a new copyright will not be granted to a work already protected once, but only to a new work. The outlawed work will be admitted as new if its appearance is changed—be it only by a few fingerings added to it. During the time the law holds, every performer and teacher considers the text as given by its author sufficient to direct him. The copyright is also a publisher's monopoly, which terminates with the law. Works still alive after that time may be printed by anybody. To prevent or circumvent this proceeding, the music publishing industry introduced editions of outlawed works adorned with more or less adequate directions by some editor or reviser. The spirit of the law is thus changed for the benefit of the publishers, while the music itself is exposed to all kinds of mischief.

There are many more annotated and "revised" editions (all different) of the same works than there are countries having a trade in printed music. In Germany each town above medium size has its own edition. The editions range from interesting, stimulating, instructive and intelligent ones to the grossest adulterations. Only a few use different print to distinguish the author's work from the handiwork of the so-called editor.

In the nineteenth century also, groups of musicians and music patrons jointly undertook the printing of those admirable sets of complete and critical editions of the works left by the great masters. These "pure" editions, financed by subscriptions and donations, are now practically unavailable, and if one has the luck to find a single volume, it is many times as expensive as the annotated editions, which are published for profit. The consequence is that most of the printed masterworks in circulation do not look as the masters intended them to look. It seems that a multitude of musicians and musical persons have never considered that somewhere an original version must exist if annotated versions abound. They do not even notice that the edition they are using is annotated or adulterated. They simply take what is handed to them—the Bulgarian edition in Sofia, the Brazilian version in Rio, and so on. This is a scandalous situation. It is not a question of worshipping the letter, but one of common decency, that every musician should insist upon having an opportunity to see musical works as their composers wanted them to be seen. All contemporary composers, even those who write rubbish get this satisfaction; Beethoven is denied it!

In order to get acquainted with the problem of the contemporary composer, I recommend Ernst Krenek's recently published book, *Music Here and Now*. Let me protest only against the silly demand on the contemporary composer (who may adore

Mozart) to write in the medium of Mozart. The distinctions between composers lie in the force of their affirmations and negations, not in the subjects they affirm or deny. Nor are they to be distinguished by the raiment they wear. This brings me to the confused but agitated talk about periods, style, folksong, national atmosphere, old instruments, and so forth. It is all typical of materialism, it is a diversion from the essential to the exterior, a facilitation of judgment, a safety-valve.

Musical productions of our civilization, regardless of time and place, have more common than contrasting traits, whether along the line of journalism or eternalism. What separates them are irrelevant peculiarities, twists, or distorted patterns. The corruption of the three-quarter measure does not express Austria, nor the Spanish way of executing a *grupetto* the soul of Spain. If it were such time-and-place specialties (or trivialities) that move us when we hear Mozart, then his lesser contemporaries could serve us just as well. Art cannot be approached like a furniture exhibition, a fancy-dress ball or a political map. Costumes in the eighteenth century were daintier than in the nineteenth, but men not weaker.

Many European folk songs were composed by individuals, most of them by professional musicians. In Russia folk songs were partly imported. The preference for minor keys here, for major keys there, must not make us believe in fundamental differences of temperament or attitude toward life. Racial conceptions of art are meaningless. We are in the greatest danger of overlooking real qualities in music if (by titles or birthplaces added to it) we are exhorted to dream, while listening, of the places and situations as we know them from books or postcards. For that purpose we might better go to harbors to stare at foreign flags and sailors.

Pleasure in old instruments, particularly of the keyboard class, is very fashionable. Candlelight is conjured up. But Mozart is better associated with the sun. Modern instruments can do almost all that the old ones can, can do much more than the old ones, and they are free from their defects. Besides, how inconsistent not to ask for pianos of the 1840's for performers of Chopin, and how paradoxical that along with a real frenzy for arrangements (such as Bach's *Chaconne* for violin solo played by one hundred men) goes a rapture for "faithfulness" to the period. (Swing at the harpsichord, which I recently saw announced, unites two periods, certainly a proof of the timeless nature of art.) It is materialism—all that—and pessimism.

The effect of music is not produced by its material —understood here as melody, rhythm, harmony— but by the treatment of it. From the first to the fifth measure compositions don't differ so much in value, particularly the tunes—at least before the coming of "atonality"—are in many cases similar. The fashion of plundering the two or four or more first measures of great music, and then continuing according to the factory pattern of the day for the fabrication of ditties, is now in full swing. It is an act not indicating poverty but laziness, for the robbers could have provided similar openings unassisted; it would only have been a bit more work. The results of such "collaboration" are liked by millions who don't know that Mozart is the honored victim, and would not know who he is if told, but if the piece were continued as Mozart wrote it—not in a factory pattern but with ever-increased inspiration in its continuation—the millions might soon stop listening, in other words, find themselves excluded, which says nothing against them.

There is no such thing as banality in material. It is always in the spirit. A piece of wood or metal or stone can be transformed into a divine message if the right spirit blesses the transformer's hand. But no means are conceivable that could incite the spirit to mass production.

Education in the old days, enjoyed mainly by those who were worthy, was intensive to a degree and yet comprehensive. Study went on all through life, but how many Bibles, how many Shakespeares have emerged? For the extensive education of the many in our plutocratic-proletarian age, one obstacle seems insurmountable. Millions of teachers are necessary. Ideally every teacher ought to be an example. And here Nature fails to provide an adequate supply, warning us, perhaps, to accept some limits.

As it is, our hypertrophic system might, I am afraid, breed an amazing average cleverness and something like many-sided ignorance, leaving us at the mercy of quackery, drugs, substitutes and artificial eccentricities, in a happiness that cannot be the true one for the human being who is privileged to be tempted and tested by problems and compelled to discriminate as an individual, who is neither a gregarious nor a rapacious animal. I see it, therefore, as the most urgent and important task for those who are deeply alarmed by the aspect of a more and more godless and loveless humanity, to defend and exercise man's best rights in the unshakable conviction that the spirit cannot be lost, nor even oppressed. And they, the forgotten men of the minority, formerly raisers and rulers, must not and probably cannot submit. They should welcome their isolation, and in this isolation pursue the ideals of simplicity, truth and nobility; they should embrace passionately the obligations implied in those virtues, for the loss of which no collective luxury can ever compensate. And, finally, they should with confident energy, also keep alive that productive skepticism which is born out of respect for the mysterious realities, giving them strength, discipline, self-respect, a widening horizon and beautiful music —a sign that they deserve it.

I hope that occasionally you may recall some of these thoughts of a musician who is eternally grateful for being one.